GREAT ARTISTS COLLECTION

Five centuries of great art in full colour

VAN GOGH

by W. UHDE

ENCYCLOPAEDIA BRITANNICA : LONDON

Volume one

COVER: *Road with Cypresses (Plate 43)*

This edition published in 1970
by Encyclopaedia Britannica International Limited, London

ISBN 0 85229 076 4

Printed in Germany

THE LIFE AND WORK OF VINCENT VAN GOGH

WHEN THE NAME OF VINCENT VAN GOGH is mentioned we are reminded of a number of brilliant pictures, but at the same time we think of the shadows of a pitiful life which its bearer dragged like a cross to an untimely Golgotha. Art and life are here so closely interwoven, so inseparably bound up with one another, that we cannot attempt to describe them separately, as is so often done in "monographs on artists". Moreover, van Gogh's life was not subordinated to the rules of any period or milieu, his work followed no one direction or programme. Both were unusual and in their way unique. The name of van Gogh suggests primarily no theme connected with the history of art, but rather an eminently human one. He was a missionary who painted. He was a painter with social ideas. His story is not that of an eye, a palette, a brush, but the tale of a lonely heart which beat within the walls of a dark prison, longing and suffering without knowing why, until one day it saw the sun, and in the sun recognized the secret of life. It flew towards it and was consumed in its rays.

This pathway from coldness to warmth, from mist to brightness, from the north to the south, had been trodden by many others before van Gogh, but in a very different way. With what dignity, what thoughtfulness and care in registering every stage did Goethe follow it! But van Gogh rushed towards the fatal glow thoughtlessly and with childlike haste, almost like a modern Icarus.

The tragedy of his brief life lies in the fact that he spent most of it seeking amidst sorrow, pain and despair after the simplest, the most obvious thing in existence, the sun, and that he died as soon as he had found it. For none of his predecessors had the way been so difficult, the transition of the northern man from the world of literature, of ideas, of morality and social problems to the sensual world of pictures. No one before him had sought so passionately after what he did not possess. One element of the southern clime was innate in his dark and frigid origin: the Mistral, that wind which can lift stones from the ground and carry them away. He had the Mistral in his heart, and borne on its wings he set out to find the rest: the sun and colour.

His life is the story of a great and passionate heart, which was entirely filled with two things: love and sorrow. Love, not in the sense of likings or preferences, of sympathy or aesthetic taste, but in its deepest form, charity, a deep religious relationship to men and things. Here is the root of his life and art. This love of his led him to self-sacrifice, to a prodigal spending of his own ego. His life was an uninterrupted giving of himself, and his painting was nothing but the most adequate means of giving himself which he discovered after many other attempts.

This impetuous devotion, this religious form of action, were in him of an unusual grandeur, and the greater they became, the harder seemed to him those words of Spinoza which in his case became a terrible truth: "He who loves God cannot expect to be loved by God in return." The violence of this love of his did not bring him within the community of men, it separated him from them and made him suspicious and lonely. Thus, together with love, a second feeling entered his heart: sorrow, not indeed in the lighter form of melancholy, but in the graver form of deep suffering and often of despair. It was interwoven into the web of his short life as an essential and inseparable part. Just as his religious love for the poor, the weak and the sick was not reciprocated, so was it also with his earthly loves. He loved three women. The first made fun of him, the second ran away from him, the third, who was really fond of him, tried to take her own life. But his last great love was for the sun, which he glorified in his pictures. Men would have nothing to do with these pictures and laughed at them. And even the sun did not love him, it robbed him of his reason and killed him.

If ever a life was tragic, Vincent's was certainly so. Only one man understood him, loved him and helped him: his brother Theo, four years his junior. At the most difficult moments Theo was always there, consoling him in his despair, suggesting new ways when he appeared to have reached an impasse, encouraging him in his creative work. Theo sacrificed his money, submitted patiently to all the unbearable, incalculable, contradictory, evil and capricious characteristics which became manifest in his elder brother as the process of self-destruction continued. Love, friendship and admiration aided him in his task. Yet one day he had to listen to the terrible words, uttered from the depths of suffering: "You can give me money, but you can't give me a wife and children."

Above the story of Vincent van Gogh's life, which lasted thirty-seven years, one might place as motto the words which he himself uttered at the death-bed of his father: "Dying is hard, but living is harder still".

Of his works, the production of which occupied barely ten years of his life, one might say what Dr. Gachet, who attended him in his last days, wrote of him: "The words 'love of art' are scarcely applicable to him, one ought to say: belief even unto martyrdom."

Vincent van Gogh was born on March 30th, 1853, at Groot-Zundert in Holland. His birthplace lay in the midst of flat country beneath a low sky, intersected by canals which might have been drawn with a ruler. The life of its inhabitants was narrow and provincial, for they were good bourgeois whose existence was easy and free from troubles; they followed the precepts of law, custom and the ten commandments. It was also considered a virtue to be "well-bred". Vincent grew up in an old-fashioned country house with many windows, in the company of a number of younger brothers and sisters. His father was a clergyman, by nature and profession helpful, good-tempered and considerate. His mother, with whom he had a great inward affinity, was named Anna-Cornelia Carbentus. The material position of the family was very modest.

The red-haired boy was not handsome. What distinguished him most in these surroundings was his temperament, which was the exact opposite of everything around him, for he was unsociable, passionate, undisciplined and retiring. A warm relationship existed from the earliest days between him and his younger brother Theo.

When he was twelve years old, he was sent to a boarding-school at Zevenbergen. At sixteen, he returned to his parents' house. His sister describes how at this time he used to escape from the tedious life of the sleepy village and take refuge in the open country to avoid the eyes of his father's inquisitive parishioners: "Broad rather than tall, his back slightly bent owing to the bad habit of letting his head hang forward, his reddish fair hair cut short beneath a straw hat, which overshadowed an unusual face: not at all the face of a boy. His brow was already slightly wrinkled, his eyebrows drawn together in deep thought across the wide forehead; his eyes small and deep-set, sometimes blue, at other times greenish, according to his changing expressions. Despite this unattractive, awkward appearance, there was yet something remarkable in his unmistakable expression of inward profundity."

Even then his parents had a feeling that there was something unusual about their son and they felt a presentiment of the trouble he would later be to them. As they walked along the lonely country road to visit the sick, they often used to stop and discuss the future of their eldest child. Their first step was to send him to The Hague, where they obtained, through the influence of his father's brother Vincent, who was connected with the firm, a post for him as salesman in the branch there of the Paris firm of Goupil. The works sold by the firm were sentimental genre paintings of the type to be seen at that time in the Paris Salon, but there were also among them lithographs of Corot's pictures. Vincent was clever at packing and unpacking books and pictures, and for three years he performed his duties in an exemplary manner. When he was twenty years old, he was sent to the London branch. There he employed his free week-ends in drawing, modestly, for his own amusement. He sent these sketches to his mother and Theo. In London he had plenty of opportunities for studying art, for seeing all kinds of works, for developing his taste. The result was disastrous. What he preferred were pictures by Mauve, Ziem, Boldini, Meissonier, Knaus, Israëls and one or two sickly religious painters. Even when names like Constable and the painters of the Barbizon school appear among his preferences, we can only conclude that he was attracted by their choice of subjects, and not by their artistic merit. At this time his artistic perceptions were obviously still unawakened, he had no feeling for class or quality; his one preoccupation was to find satisfaction in the contents of the pictures.

The inward peace of mind in which he then lived was broken when he fell in love with the daughter of his landlady, a widow named Loyer. This girl led him on and finally told him that she was already engaged. The neurasthenic condition into which this adventure plunged him was not without subsequent effects on his relations with the Goupil Galleries, both in London, where he was dismissed, and in Paris, where he obtained another post through his connection—after a short unhappy stay at home and another visit to London. He was tactless in his dealings with customers, whose taste he criticized and who did not want to be served by the 'Dutch peasant'. Nor were his employers pleased when he informed them that trade was nothing but organized theft. In Paris he remained for two months, and then, after another short visit to London, he spent the years 1875 and 1876 in the French capital. Although he continued to work at Goupil's his attitude to artistic matters had changed. He did not like his work, was not interested in the beautiful city, which gave him nothing, and lodged in a room in Montmartre, where he read the Bible with a young Englishman, discussing its contents for hours on end. He often went to the English Church, and thought of devoting his life to the poor. The result was that he finally left Goupil's for good.

His anxious father came to Paris and made proposals which did not meet with Vincent's approval. Theo advised him to become a painter, but even this idea, which had occupied Vincent's mind earlier at one moment in London, was now rejected. His education was superficial and chaotic, and he was not suited to any ordinary profession. In 1876 he went back to London and obtained a post *au pair* at Ramsgate, as French teacher in a school owned by a grotesque pedant, who had about twenty pale and underfed boarders in his house. Vincent had to collect the school fees from the parents, who lived in Whitechapel, and thus gained an insight into the housing conditions of the poor. He lost his job when he returned without having got the money. Then he went to London to the house of a Methodist preacher, who kept a rather better boarding-school and with whom he had eager discussions on religious matters. He himself preached bad sermons, and when he was ill, he praised illness and found sorrow better than joy. The idea of consoling those who are unfortunate in this world became stronger and stronger in his mind.

Christmas of this year he spent in Etten, where his parents were now living. He was gloomy and restless, and they breathed a sigh of relief when he went away again. Through his uncle Vincent he obtained a post as apprentice in a bookshop at Dordrecht. At this period he lived like an ascetic, wore Quaker clothes and gave himself up entirely to piety. Despite these sorrowful and gloomy moods he still took an interest in the landscape surrounding him, which sometimes found enthusiastic expression, and we may assume that now and then he made sketches of it. But at this time drawing was probably no more to him than the song a traveller whistles as he tramps alone along a dusty country road. How poor his understanding for art then was, is proved by the fact that in the small town museum a trashy Christ in the Garden of Gethsemane by Ary Scheffer was the only thing to excite his admiration.

He did not stay long in Dordrecht. He was now determined to become a pastor. For this a university degree was necessary, and first he had to fill in the gaps in his education and sit for an examination. He lived in Amsterdam with an uncle of his who was an admiral and who alienated him by his martial bearing. For fourteen months Vincent worked perseveringly, and we find him spending the hot summer afternoons struggling with Greek dictionaries. But he could not manage it; he withdrew from the examination and decided to become a preacher on his own account. He left Amsterdam and went to prepare himself at the evangelical mission school in Brussels. After three months it was found impossible to give him a definite appointment, but he was allowed to go as an independent missionary on his own account and at his own risk to the Borinage, a coal-mining district. He went to Pâturages, a village near Mons, that same Mons where Verlaine had been imprisoned only three years before. Then he received an appointment for six months in the neighbouring village of Wasmes. Taking the lives of the early Christians as a model, he gave everything he possessed to the poor, went about in a worn soldier's coat, wore no stockings, made his own shirts out of old pack-cloth, and slept on the ground in a wooden hut. He looked after the miners when they returned exhausted after twelve hours' work underground, or when they had been injured by explosions in the pits; he helped the sick during an epidemic of typhus. He preached too, but he had not the gift of speaking. He devoted himself entirely to his work, ate bad food, became weak and thin. But he would not give up half-way. His father, although he was himself a clergyman, could not understand this eccentric behaviour; he came to see him, pacified the wayward son with whom it had pleased God to burden him, and took lodgings for him at a baker's. Even the religious body which had given him the appointment were appalled at his "excess of zeal", and recalled him under the pretext that his sermons were not good enough.

It is characteristic of the contradictions in his nature that his first pictures date from this very time when he could exclaim: "Christ was the greatest of all artists", and that it was then that he spoke a great deal about painting and wrote to his brother: "I often long to go back to pictures." He did a number of water-colours and drawings of the life of the miners. Now began the struggle between his religious aspirations and his artistic tendencies, which he was unable to reconcile. When the latter finally won the victory, it was only after many inward struggles and terrible relapses.

Returning to Etten, he found consolation in his father, and painted flowers, which he had always loved. But a short time afterwards he went back again to the black country and wandered about the roads with bleeding feet, half saviour, half tramp, sleeping in the open air: when he arrived back in the Borinage his despair knew no bounds. Then suddenly the other tendency asserted itself; he wanted to become a painter, he spent all his time drawing, and he wrote to his brother, who was at Goupil's in Paris, that he wanted to get out of this "dreadful, very dreadful cage". He appealed to their mutual, very sincere affection and regained his brother's confidence. They met at Etten. Vincent spent the winter in Brussels drawing and studying in the Museum. It was now 1881 and he was twenty-eight years old. Then an unfortunate love affair with a cousin at his home once more disturbed his peace of mind.

Vincent next went to The Hague, where he remained for two years. He painted in the house of his cousin Mauve, in whose pictures the same flocks of sheep were still to be seen. But this relationship gave Vincent no satisfaction. Visits to the Mauritshuis contributed to his artistic education. One may suppose that here for the first time a feeling for quality showed itself in him, that it was no longer the social element, the religious legend, which interested him, when he stood long before the pictures of Rembrandt. He was on the right path, but at the beginning of 1882 an event occurred which plunged him back into the depths of self-abasement. He got to know a drunken woman who had spent her life in a state of moral and physical misery. He brought her and her children to live in his house and used her as a model. She drank and smoked cigars while he went hungry. There is a sketch by him, called "Sorrow", in which we see her crouching hopelessly on the ground, with withered breasts. What were his real feelings for this woman is clear from the quotation from Michelet which he wrote on the sketch: "How can there be lonely, deserted women in the world?" This relapse into the sphere of religious and social ideas lasted eighteen months. Once again it was Theo who came and set him free. It was difficult for Vincent after this experience to rediscover his intimate connection with the brighter realms of art. He began to wander about and came to Drenthe, a lonely, impoverished place. It seems that here he felt the first symptoms of madness. The cross which he had taken up of his own free will, first in the Borinage and now with this woman, had borne him down to the ground. At the end it seemed as if he could not rise again. In the religious sense he had perhaps reached a wonderful climax, but from the worldly point of view, that is to say as understood by all good citizens and pastors, it was an unbridgeable gulf. He dragged himself back to his parents' house, defeated, a prodigal son who had wasted the treasures of his heart in orgies of misery, in a drunken feast of self-sacrifice.

In Nuenen, where his parents were now living, he regained strength enough to pull himself together and resume painting in an atelier which he had fitted up in a church. His sister describes his appearance at this time: "Carelessly dressed in the blue smock of a Flemish peasant, his hair cut short, his reddish-brown beard unkempt, his eyes often inflamed and red from staring at some object in the sunlight, his hat with its soft brim pressed right down over his eyes." Another unhappy love-affair came to disturb him, and in addition to this, in the year 1885 his father died.

Vincent now spent all his time painting: the deep sky, the wide plains, the low houses of the country. He painted in dark, heavy colours which even at this time he was fond of contrasting and weighing against one another. The figures and land in these paintings were Dutch. He had been reading Zola and his love for the land had been strengthened thereby. At this time Daumier had significance for him, probably because he liked his dark prevailing tone, and perhaps also because a human and social element was manifest in his works. The worthy Breitner had taught him to paint "well", in the sense of the old Dutch masters. Nuenen denotes the first period of his art; what had gone before need not be considered. But this art remained "provincial" and through it he could never have achieved eternal fame. The most typical picture from this period is the "Potato-eaters". If we compare it with Le Nain's pictures of peasants, we obtain an idea of how much was still to be done.

Now he proceeded by rapid stages towards his artistic maturity. He had little time to lose. Only six years remained until his death. The first stage in the journey was Antwerp, where he arrived when he was thirty-one years old. The gay and varied life of the city filled him with pleasure. He attended the painting classes at the Academy, but his colours dripped from the canvas to the floor. "Who are you?" asked the indignant teacher. "I am Vincent the Dutchman," he shouted back, and was transferred to the drawing class. In Antwerp he was able to study works of Rubens and the Japanese artists. Under their influence he gave up using dark colours; his palette became lighter. The study of Hokusai's "Hundred Views of Fujiyama" gave his pencil accuracy and style.

After three months he had exhausted Antwerp. In February, 1886, Theo, who was still at Goupil's, received a note from his brother fixing a rendezvous in the Salon Carré at the Louvre. The two brothers went to live together. Vincent worked at Cormon's atelier, where he got to know Toulouse-Lautrec and the young Emile Bernard, with whom he remained afterwards in close touch and maintained an interesting correspondence. Up till now he had only known the Dutch painters, and among the French only Millet, Daumier, the Barbizon school, Monticelli. Now he saw Delacroix and the Impressionists. Manet had been dead for three years, but the others were at the height of their careers and of their art. And they were the centres of attraction. At Goupil's he made the acquaintance of Gauguin and saw pictures by Degas which he did not like. More interesting for him was Père Tanguy's shop, where paintings by Pissarro, Cézanne, Renoir, Sisley, Seurat, Guillaumin and Signac were to be found. He got to know these painters and took part in the discussions they held in the shop. Here were revelations for him: light, colour, a new technique. That of Seurat influenced him especially. He saw with different eyes, absorbed and learned. With his brother he soon moved to Rue Lepick, where they had a view of the Moulin de la Galette and their little restaurant, kept by Mère Bataille, where besides themselves Mendès, Willette and Jaurès took their meals. Vincent soon left Cormon's atelier. He worked in the streets, at Montmartre, in the environs of Paris, at Chatou, Bougival and Suresnes. He painted the little restaurants in the bright colours of spring, in bright blue and pink. He painted the yellow still-life with the candle and the sealed letter, he painted Père Tanguy and other portraits. Paris awakened and liberated his sensuality. Only rarely, as in the celebrated "Courtyard of a Prison", did a more thoughtful social note appear.

But the winter was hard. There came bad moods and crises of neurasthenia. Then too it suddenly became clear that in reality everything was in vain, that these pictures could not be sold. Despite his influential position at Goupil's, Theo was unable to sell a single one of his brother's pictures. There were many quarrels, and the atmosphere became unbearable.

To all the other reasons which induced Vincent to leave Paris must be added this: a subconscious realization that this city was not for him an end and a goal in itself, but only the penultimate stage before that for which all that had gone before had been merely preparation. The Impressionists? Certainly, he used their modes of expression, saw with their eyes, employed their technique; both he and they were inspired by the same Japanese school. But beyond that? They loved the appearance of things and loved them with well-tempered bourgeois hearts. He loved passionately the things themselves. They liked brightness. He was a fanatical worshipper of the sun. That was something different, something deeper. He now set out to devote himself to this service of the sun, which was to be the justification of the whole of his previous life. One day his brother found on the table an affectionate letter of farewell.

In February, 1888, he arrived at Arles. He took a room in a small hotel, which had a café beneath it. We know from his pictures this room with the narrow bed and the two straw chairs, and we know also the café with the billiard table in the middle and the three lamps hanging like suns from the ceiling, while the terrace of the café appears in one of his finest sketches. He painted and drew every day without a pause. He painted the squares and streets of the town, the Aliscamps, the public gardens, the bridge, sunsets over Arles, fields with the railway in the background. He painted the blossoms of the fruit trees, gardens with gaily-coloured flowers. He painted white roses in a vase, lemons in a basket; he painted portraits, his own time after time, the Berceuse, the Arlésienne, the Zouave, the peasants of the Camargue, the postman Roulin, who was his crony and with whom he used to sit in the little café until late into the night. He went to Les Saintes-Maries-de-la-Mer and painted the sea and the boats. He painted and painted . . . Here in Arles he made himself immortal, he created his work, his *monumentum aere perennius*, the work not of an eye, a palette, a hand, but of a great and generous heart. Only occasionally, when his heart was tired, his hand went on painting, and then empty or decorative elements entered into a few among these hundreds of pictures.

He gave himself completely and lavishly, as he had once done in the Borinage. He rented a house, painted it yellow and adorned it with six pictures of sunflowers. It was to be the "House of the Friends". The idea of the communal life of the early Christians kept returning to his mind; he dreamed of artists living together, producing the most beautiful pictures as the fruit of their existence in common.

He remained the deep, sensitive man he had been before. He had not become a "bourgeois", nor did he become a "painter". Something "sentimental", in the widest and loftiest sense of the word, is the essential element in his art. If we wish to analyse his work, we must begin with these values of feeling and expression. He was a lover who penetrated from the surface into the essence, the totality of things. He did not love sunshine: he loved the sun; and it was the latter he wanted to paint, not the former. When he writes: "how beautiful is yellow", this is not merely the sensual reaction of a painter, but the confession of a man for whom yellow was the colour of the sun, a symbol of warmth and light. Yellow aroused ecstasy first as an idea in the man, then as a colour in the artist. Thus the sunflowers which he painted rise above the significance of ordinary still-life, and he himself says that they produce an effect like that of stained-glass windows in Gothic churches.

In his portraits, especially in his self-portraits, these values of feeling and expression are to be found in abundance. He himself confessed that he would have preferred above all things to paint pictures of saints, with modern figures it is true, but intimately related to the primitive Christians. But he was afraid of his own emotions. His landscapes too are not reflections of an eye, but actual experiences of a human being. He himself says of them that in one he wished to express great peace, in another the extremes of loneliness and sorrow. His religious attitude to the world is perhaps most vividly expressed when he paints flowers. His sister wrote of him that even when he was a boy he understood the "soul" of flowers. He used to tie them together in bundles with a sensitive hand, the same hand with which later he packed books and pictures into cases, and later still tended the wounds of the sick. With this same delicate hand his brush now reproduced not only the appearance but the very soul of flowers. In one of his letters he speaks of the "sickly greenish-pink smile of the last flower of autumn". That is the language of a conception which is the direct opposite of that of the Impressionists.

But these values of feeling and expression, which are the first we must note in his pictures, are not mere illustration or literature transferred to canvas, but take their place with the other features of his work and form a dominant note which is expressed with the pure means of painting. Of the other plastic values we must mention his understanding for space. He knew how to give an exact impression of distances, not only by means of houses and trees, or by inconspicuous points of contact such as a little cart which—as in the picture of the railway—he places in the middle of the plane, but even by means of the varying forms of furrows in a field.

That the values of movement also play an important role in his works is likewise not surprising when we consider his passionate temperament. It is characteristic that he chose as subjects for copies Rembrandt's Raising of Lazarus, Delacroix's Good Samaritan, Daumier's Drinkers, and Millet's Sower, all of them works containing great energy of gesture. The Mistral which never ceased raging in his heart drove him into the open air to face that Provençal Mistral which could bow trees and crops down to earth. Thus was created in the struggle between these forces the "style flamboyant" of those pictures of driving clouds and rustling cypresses.

In making everything comprehensive become reality he was helped by those tactile values which are present in such abundance. He had two ways of realizing his feeling for tangibility: either, like the Japanese, inserting with the most exact draughtsmanship every little detail of ground, boats, rain, sea, etc., or else, on the contrary, by simplifying everything, by omitting the details and only suggesting, as Giotto used to do, the essential form and material of houses, mountains and trees. "I have tried to retain in the drawing what is essential", he wrote to Emile Bernard, and in the same letter he says that he fills in with simplified colours the surfaces rounded by the outlines. In this way many of his pictures have an exactitude and probability which surpass those of nature.

These values taken together make up the style which is typical of his work. But more than by all these features, we recognize his works by the colour values. His letters from Arles to Emile Bernard with their descriptions of colouring abound in the praise of Veronese green, light green, yellow in all its shades from orange to light lemon-yellow, Prussian blue, vermilion, violet and pink. These colours, in which he revels, he places together, contrasts, or combines to form harmonies by the addition of others. A young painter to whom he once gave advice relates that van Gogh was always comparing painting to music, and that he took piano lessons from an old organist in order to determine which tones of the instrument corresponded to Prussian blue, sapphire green, cadmium and yellow-ochre.

The beauty of pure colours and their harmonious blending in van Gogh's works has never been surpassed. It is the beauty and grandeur of nature itself, the equivalent of that which God has created in birds, butterflies, flowers and stones, that beauty which exalts us and fills us with joy. All these colours and harmonies occur in nature just as he paints them or in a similar form. Van Gogh, however, was unable to find sources of inspiration higher than these; they were the limits of his art.

"Oh, the beautiful sun of midsummer! It beats upon my head, and I do not doubt that it makes one a little queer", wrote van Gogh from Arles. His invitations to visit the "House of Friends" had been accepted only by Gauguin. They spoke a great deal about art, Gauguin assuming a didactic tone which accentuated the morbid irritability of the other until it reached a crisis. It appears that van Gogh threw a glass at his friend's head and on another occasion threatened him with a razor. What is certain is that in a moment of mental derangement he cut off his own ear, wrapped it in paper and left it about three o'clock in the morning at a brothel. While Gauguin left Arles as quickly as he could, van Gogh was taken to hospital, where his disease took the form of hallucinations. His brother came to visit him there. After a fortnight he became calm again and was able to leave the hospital. But the inhabitants of Arles presented a petition stating that as a dangerous madman he ought not to be left in liberty. He returned to the hospital, and during the next few weeks created some beautiful pictures: several self-portraits, among them the one showing him with his severed ear, the garden of the hospital, the inner room with the stove, the beds and curtains. Signac visited him at this time, and they were allowed to go out together, as far as van Gogh's house. This short visit wore him out. He himself realized that he would have to go to an asylum, and accordingly he went to that of Saint-Rémy, a few miles away, where he was given two rooms, one of which he used as an atelier. Here he painted a number of wonderful pictures of everything that surrounded him: the house and the garden seen from all angles, landscapes seen from the open window, with cypresses and olive trees, more self-portraits, the doctor, the attendant. The last intoxication of southern colour came upon him. His letters to Emile Bernard at this time are filled with countless observations on colouring. Here he created some of his maturest and most beautiful works, the copies made from reproductions after Rembrandt, Delacroix, Daumier and Millet. The zenith of his artistic achievement coincided with his first successes. The *Mercure de France* published an appreciative article on his painting and Theo was able to announce what seemed impossible, that he had sold a picture.

In Saint-Rémy peace once more entered into his soul. His clarity of mind and resignation were such that with painful humour he compared the living-room in bad weather to the third-class waiting-room of a remote village station, because some of the patients always wore their hats, carried walking-sticks and were attired in travelling dress. Nevertheless fresh crises repeatedly afflicted him and during one of these he swallowed a quantity of paints. The sojourn in Saint-Rémy became intolerable to him and at his brother's suggestion he decided to go to Auvers-sur-Oise and place himself in the care of Dr. Gachet, a friend of impressionistic painters and their works. On May 18th, 1890, he arrived in Paris, where his healthy appearance and cheerful mien were remarked upon. Three days later he reached his destination. Dr. Gachet's friendly attitude and admiration of his art made his stay there a pleasant one and were the prelude to another period of intense creative activity. He painted the banks of the Oise, three large pictures with wide-spreading cornfields, the celebrated picture of the little Mairie at Auvers, with a palette determined by the atmosphere of the Ile-de-France. He also painted a portrait of Dr. Gachet and several others. This was the last impetuous effort of his life. "I will give you back the money or give away my soul", he wrote to his brother.

On July 27th he borrowed a revolver on the pretext that he wanted to shoot crows, went into the fields, leaned against the trunk of a tree and shot himself in the breast. "Misery will never end", was one of the last things he said to his brother.

Theo followed him to the grave six months later. They are buried side by side in the little churchyard of Auvers-sur-Oise.

LIST OF PLATES

All works are oil paintings except where otherwise stated. The numbers at the end of each entry refer to J.-B. de la Faille, *Vincent van Gogh,* revised edition 1970. Measurements in inches.

1. PORTRAIT OF PÈRE TANGUY. 1887. Paris, Musée Rodin. (F 363)   36¼ × 29½

2. FLOWERS IN A COPPER VASE. 1886. Paris, Louvre. (F 213)   29 × 23¾

3. SELF-PORTRAIT. 1887. Amsterdam, Vincent van Gogh Museum. (F344)   17¼ × 14¾

4. BASKET WITH APPLES. 1887. Otterlo, Kröller-Müller Museum. (F 378)   19¾ × 24

5. VAN GOGH'S HOUSE AT ARLES. September 1888. Amsterdam, Vincent van Gogh Museum. (F464)   30 × 37

6. THE RESTAURANT DE LA SIRÈNE AT ASNIÈRES. 1887. Paris, Louvre. (F313)   22½ × 26¾

7. CORNFIELD. 1887. Amsterdam, Vincent van Gogh Museum. (F 310)   21¼ × 25½

8. MARKET GARDENS. June 1888. Amsterdam, Vincent van Gogh Museum. (F 412)   28½ × 36¼

9. THE ALISCAMPS AT ARLES. November 1888. Otterlo, Kröller-Müller Museum. (F 486)   28¾ × 36¼

10. THE DRAWBRIDGE. Watercolour. 1888. Zürich, Kunsthaus (on loan). (F 1480)   11¾ × 11¾

11. THE ZOUAVE. June 1888. New York, Mrs. Albert D. Lasker. (F 424)   32 × 25½

12. GIRL ON PINK BACKGROUND. May 1888. Otterlo, Kröller-Müller Museum. (F 518)   20 × 19¼

13. FLOWERING ALMOND TWIG. February 1888. Amsterdam, Vincent van Gogh Museum. (F 392)   9½ × 7½

14. SUNFLOWERS. August 1888. London, National Gallery. (F 454)   36¼ × 28½

15. THE PAINTER ON HIS WAY TO WORK. August 1888. Formerly Magdeburg, Kaiser-Friedrich Museum. (F 448)   19 × 17¼

16. PORTRAIT OF EUGÈNE BOCH. September 1888. Paris, Louvre. (F 462)   23½ × 17¾

17. SELF-PORTRAIT. 1888. Amsterdam, Vincent van Gogh Museum. (F 522)   25½ × 20

18. THE DRAWBRIDGE. March 1888. Amsterdam, Vincent van Gogh Museum. (F 400)   23 × 28¾

19. BOATS AT LES SAINTES-MARIES. Watercolour. June 1888. Berlin, Bernhard Koehler. (F 1429)   15¼ × 21¼

20. BOATS ON THE RHÔNE. August 1888. Essen, Folkwang Museum. (F 449)   21¾ × 26

21. STILL LIFE WITH COFFEE-POT. May 1888. France, Marquise de Chabannes. (F 410)   25½ × 32

22. LA MOUSMÉ. July 1888. Washington, D.C., National Gallery of Art (Chester Dale Collection). (F 431)   29 × 23½

23. CAFÉ AT NIGHT. September 1888. Otterlo, Kröller-Müller Museum. (F 467)   32 × 25¾

24. THE YELLOW CHAIR WITH PIPE. December 1888. London, Tate Gallery. (F 498)   36½ × 28¾

25. GAUGUIN'S ARMCHAIR. December 1888. Amsterdam, Vincent van Gogh Museum. (F 499)   35¾ × 28½

26. PORTRAIT OF AN ACTOR. 1888. Otterlo, Kröller-Müller Museum. (F 533)   25½ × 21½

27. PORTRAIT OF ARMAND ROULIN. November 1888. Rotterdam, Boymans-van Beuningen Museum. (F 493)   25½ × 21¼

28. THE SOWER. October 1888. Amsterdam, Vincent van Gogh Museum. (F 451)
$12\frac{1}{2} \times 15\frac{3}{4}$

29. VIEW OF ARLES. April 1889. Munich, Neue Staatsgalerie. (F 516) $28\frac{1}{2} \times 36\frac{1}{4}$

30. THE POSTMAN ROULIN. February 1889. Otterlo, Kröller-Müller Museum. (F 439) $25\frac{1}{2} \times 21\frac{1}{4}$

31. 'LA BERCEUSE' (MME ROULIN). February 1889. Otterlo, Kröller-Müller Museum. (F 504) $36\frac{1}{4} \times 28\frac{3}{4}$

32. THE ENCLOSED FIELD. November 1889. Otterlo, Kröller-Müller Museum. (F 720) $28\frac{1}{4} \times 36\frac{1}{4}$

33. STILL LIFE WITH DRAWING-BOARD. January 1889. Otterlo, Kröller-Müller Museum. (F 604) $19\frac{3}{4} \times 25\frac{1}{4}$

34. LANDSCAPE NEAR AUVERS. July 1890. Munich, Neue Staatsgalerie. (F 782) $29 \times 36\frac{1}{4}$

35. ROWING-BOATS. 1890. Detroit, Institute of Arts. (F 798) $28\frac{1}{2} \times 36\frac{1}{4}$

36. MOUNTAIN LANDSCAPE. May 1890. Otterlo, Kröller-Müller Museum. (F 724) $23\frac{1}{4} \times 28\frac{1}{4}$

37. THE RAVINE. December 1889. Otterlo, Kröller-Müller Museum. (F 661) $28\frac{1}{4} \times 36\frac{1}{4}$

38. CHILD WITH ORANGE. June 1890. Winterthur, Mrs. L. Jäggli-Hahnloser. (F 785) $19\frac{3}{4} \times 20$

39. TWO CHILDREN. June 1890. Formerly Erlenbach-Zürich, Richard Kisling. (F 784) $20\frac{1}{4} \times 18\frac{1}{4}$

40. PINE TREES. November 1889. Otterlo, Kröller-Müller Museum. (F 652) $36\frac{1}{4} \times 28\frac{3}{4}$

41. PORTRAIT OF DR. GACHET. June 1890. New York, S. Kramarsky Trust Fund. (F 753) $26 \times 22\frac{1}{2}$

42. IRISES. May 1890. Amsterdam, Vincent van Gogh Museum. (F 678) $36\frac{1}{4} \times 29$

43. ROAD WITH CYPRESSES. May 1890. Otterlo, Kröller-Müller Museum. (F 683) $36\frac{1}{4} \times 28\frac{3}{4}$

44. CROWS OVER A CORNFIELD. July 1890. Amsterdam, Vincent van Gogh Museum. (F 779) $19\frac{3}{4} \times 39\frac{1}{2}$

45. MEADOW WITH BUTTERFLIES. May 1890. London, National Gallery. (F 672) $25\frac{1}{4} \times 32$

46. DAUBIGNY'S GARDEN. June 1890. Amsterdam, Vincent van Gogh Museum. (F 765) 20×20

47. SELF-PORTRAIT. May 1890. Paris, Louvre. (F 627) $25\frac{1}{2} \times 21\frac{1}{4}$

48. VAN GOGH'S BEDROOM AT ARLES. September 1889. Amsterdam, Vincent van Gogh Museum. (F 482) $28\frac{1}{4} \times 35\frac{1}{2}$

1. *PORTRAIT OF PÈRE TANGUY.* 1887. Paris, Musée Rodin

2. *FLOWERS IN A COPPER VASE*. 1886. Paris, Louvre

3. *SELF-PORTRAIT*. 1887. Amsterdam, Vincent van Gogh Museum

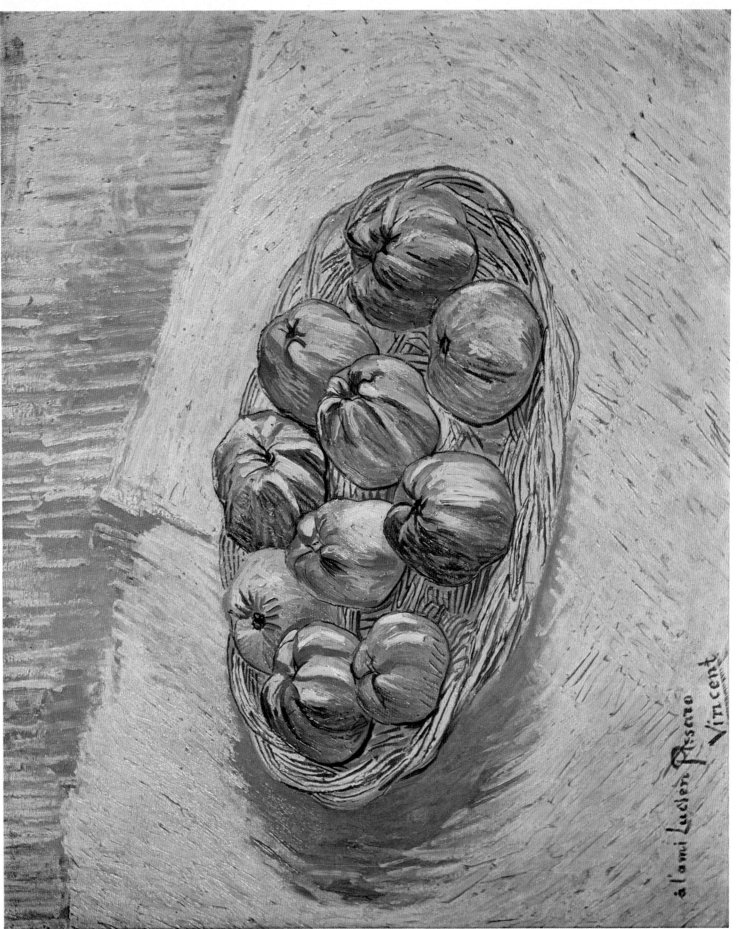

4. *BASKET WITH APPLES.* 1887. Otterlo, Kröller-Müller Museum

5. *VAN GOGH'S HOUSE AT ARLES*. September 1888. Amsterdam, Vincent van Gogh Museum

6. *THE RESTAURANT DE LA SIRÈNE AT ASNIÈRES*. 1887. Paris, Louvre

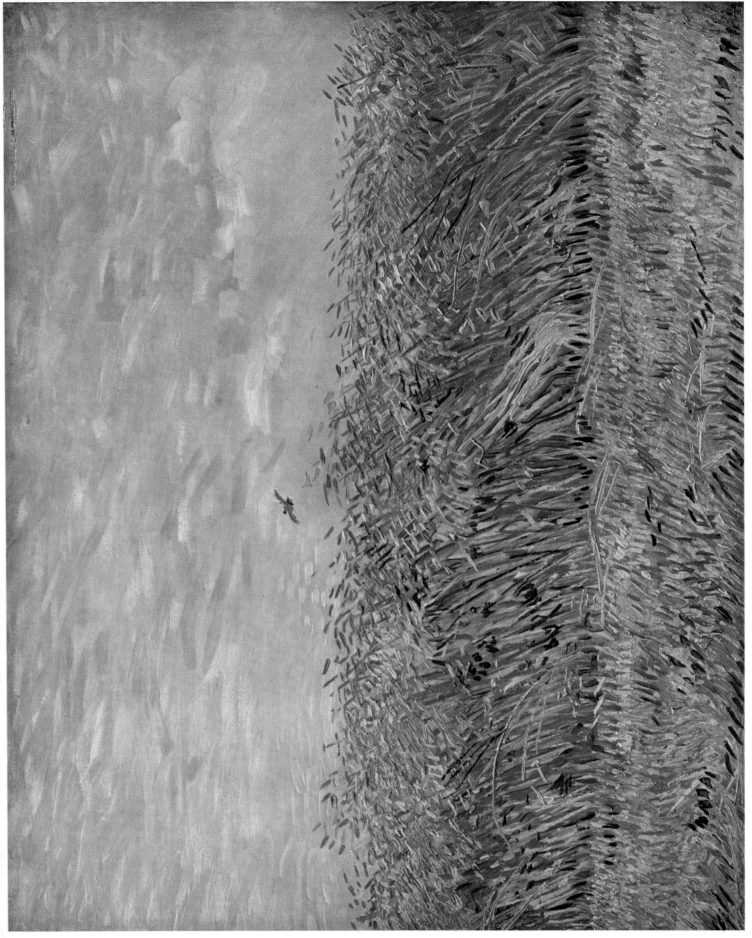

7. *CORNFIELD*. 1887. Amsterdam, Vincent van Gogh Museum

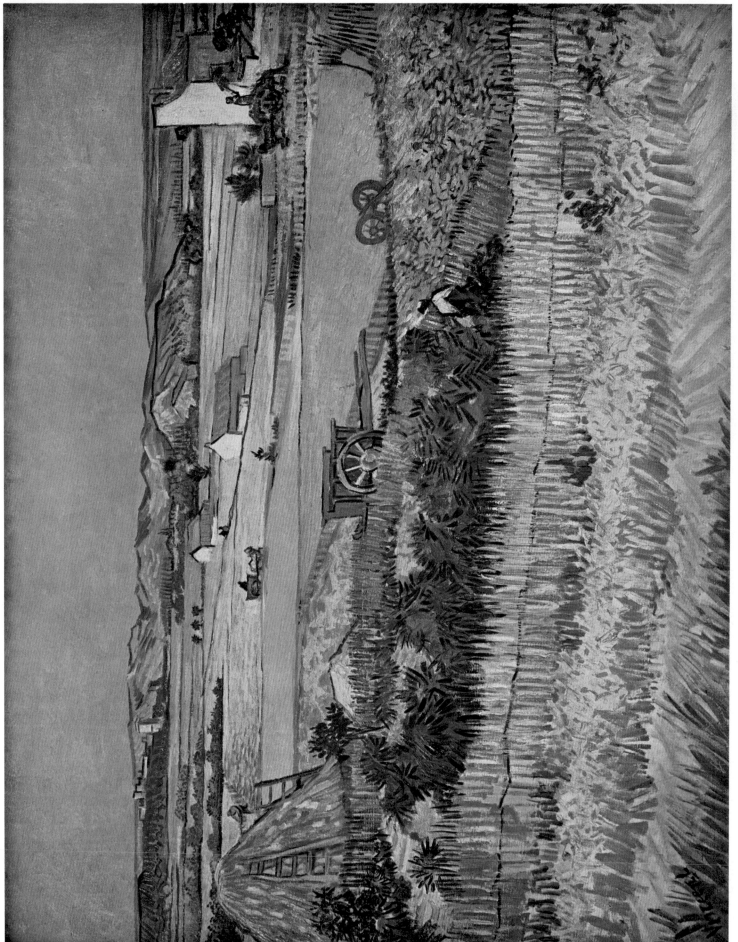

8. *MARKET GARDENS*. June 1888. Amsterdam, Vincent van Gogh Museum

10. *THE DRAWBRIDGE*. Watercolour, 1888. Zürich, Kunsthaus (on loan)

11. *THE ZOUAVE.* June 1888. New York, Mrs. Albert D. Lasker

12. *GIRL ON PINK BACKGROUND*. May 1888. Otterlo, Kröller-Müller Museum

13. *FLOWERING ALMOND TWIG*. February 1888. Amsterdam, Vincent van Gogh Museum

14. *SUNFLOWERS.* August 1888. London, National Gallery

15. *THE PAINTER ON HIS WAY TO WORK*. August 1888. Formerly Magdeburg, Kaiser-Friedrich Museum

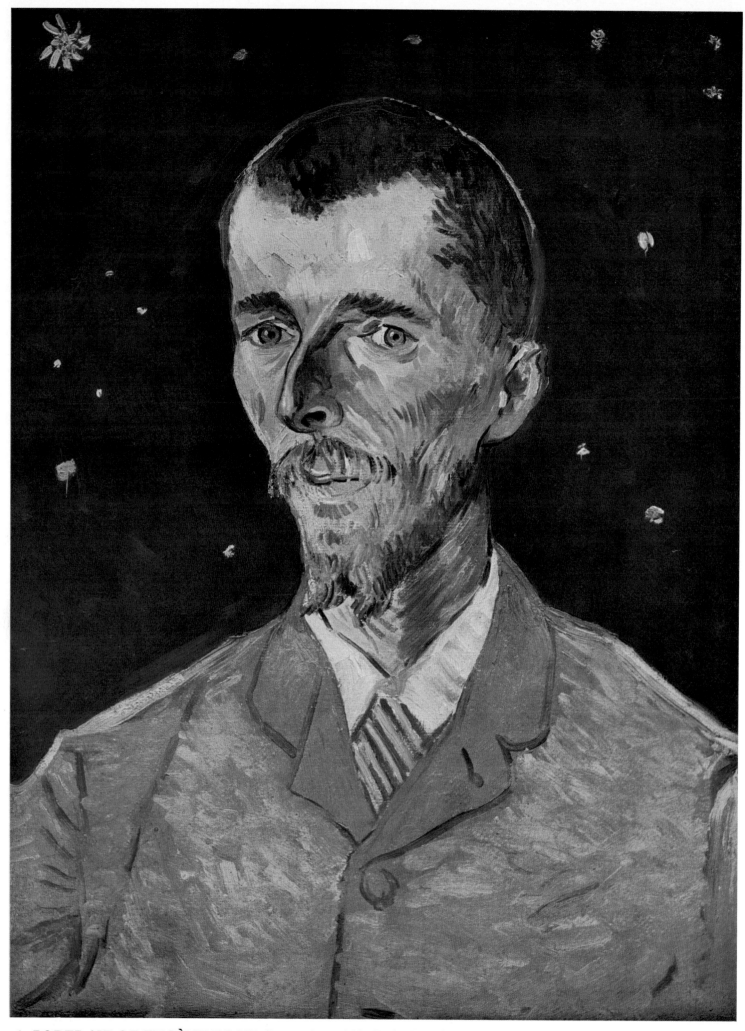

16. *PORTRAIT OF EUGÈNE BOCH*. September 1888. Paris, Louvre

17. *SELF-PORTRAIT*. 1888. Amsterdam, Vincent van Gogh Museum

18. *THE DRAWBRIDGE*. March 1888. Amsterdam, Vincent van Gogh Museum

19. *BOATS AT LES SAINTES-MARIES*. Watercolour, June 1888. Berlin, Bernhard Koehler

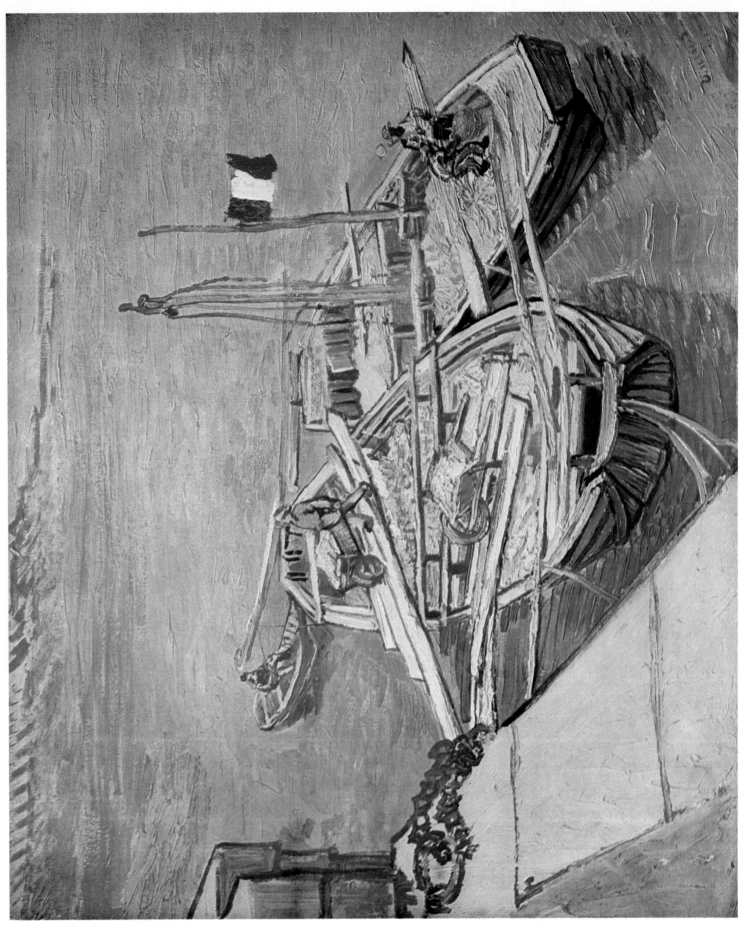

20. *BOATS ON THE RHÔNE*. August 1888. Essen, Folkwang Museum.

22. *LA MOUSMÉ.* July 1888. Washington D.C., National Gallery of Art (Chester Dale Collection)

23. *CAFÉ AT NIGHT*. September 1888. Otterlo, Kröller-Müller Museum

24. *THE YELLOW CHAIR WITH PIPE*. December 1888. London, Tate Gallery

25. *GAUGUIN'S ARMCHAIR*. December 1888. Amsterdam, Vincent van Gogh Museum

26. *PORTRAIT OF AN ACTOR.* 1888. Otterlo, Kröller-Müller Museum

27. *PORTRAIT OF ARMAND ROULIN*. 1888. Rotterdam, Boymans-van Beuningen Museum

28. *THE SOWER*. October 1888. Amsterdam, Vincent van Gogh Museum

29. *VIEW OF ARLES*. April 1889. Munich, Neue Staatsgalerie

30. *THE POSTMAN ROULIN.* February 1889. Otterlo, Kröller-Müller Museum

31. '*LA BERCEUSE*' *(MME ROULIN)*. February 1889. Otterlo, Kröller-Müller Museum

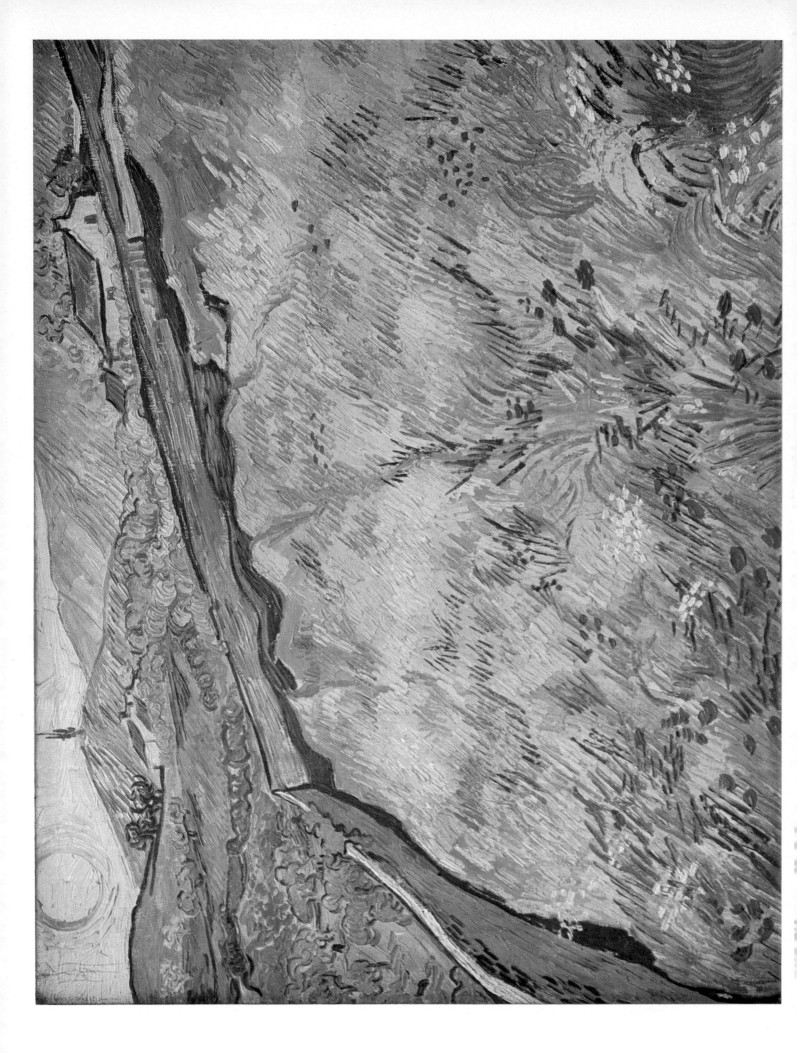

33. *STILL LIFE WITH DRAWING-BOARD*. January 1889. Otterlo, Kröller-Müller Museum

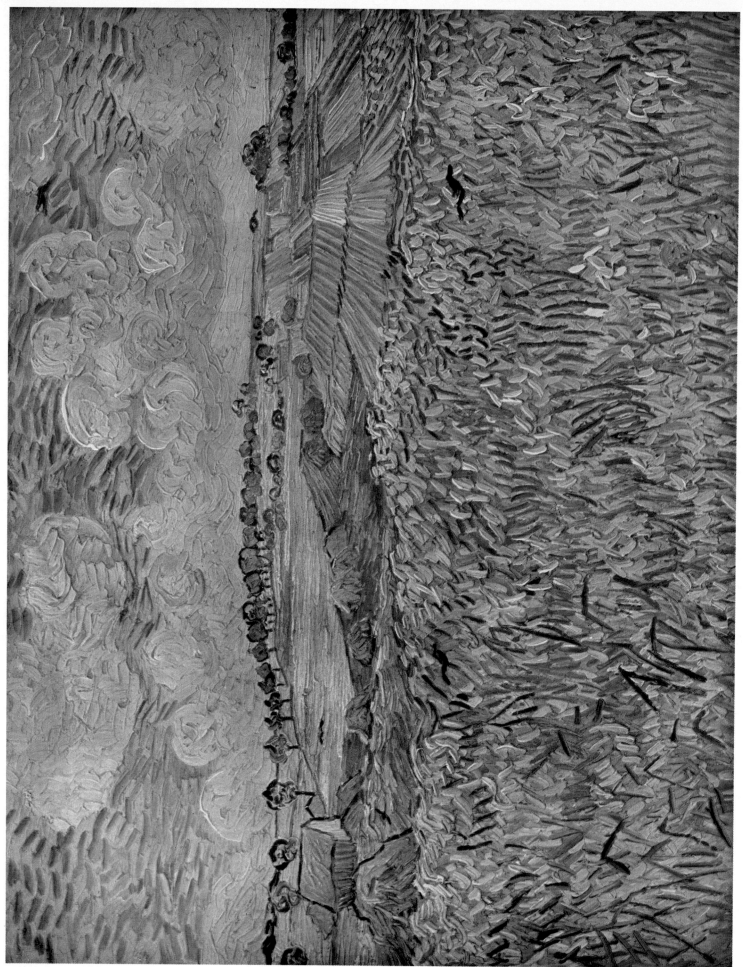

34. *LANDSCAPE NEAR AUVERS.* July 1890. Munich, Neue Staatsgalerie

36. *MOUNTAIN LANDSCAPE.* May 1890. Otterlo, Kröller-Müller Museum

37. *THE RAVINE*. December 1889. Otterlo, Kröller-Müller Museum

38. *CHILD WITH ORANGE*. June 1890. Winterthur, Mrs. L. Jäggli-Hahnloser

39. *TWO CHILDREN*. June 1890. Formerly Erlenbach-Zürich, Richard Kisling

40. *PINE TREES*. November 1889. Otterlo, Kröller-Müller Museum

41. *PORTRAIT OF DR. GACHET.* June 1890. New York, S. Kramarsky Trust Fund

42. *IRISES*. May 1890. Amsterdam, Vincent van Gogh Museum

43. *ROAD WITH CYPRESSES*. May 1890. Otterlo, Kröller-Müller Museum

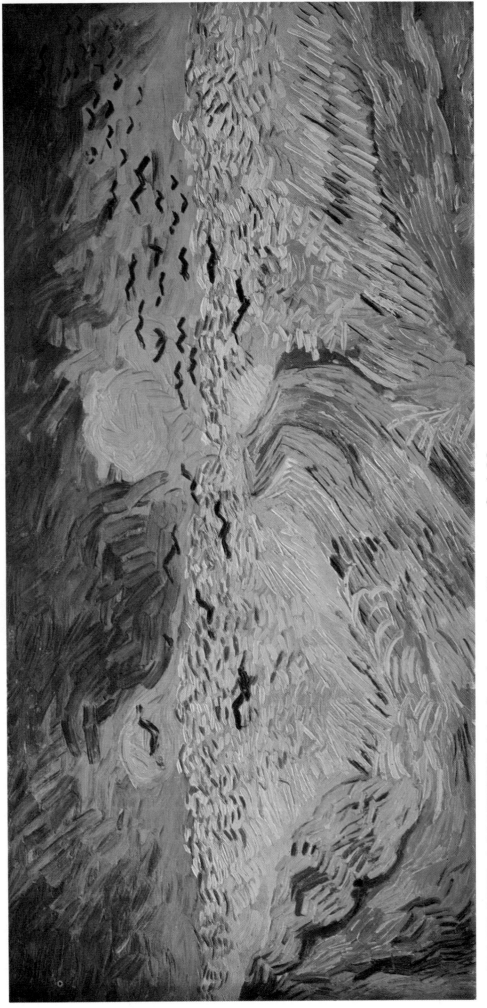

44. *CROWS OVER A CORNFIELD*. July 1890. Amsterdam, Vincent van Gogh Museum

46. *DAUBIGNY'S GARDEN*. June 1890. Amsterdam, Vincent van Gogh Museum

47. *SELF-PORTRAIT*. May 1890. Paris Louvre